In a day when th dominion, nothing could be more timely than Candi MacAlpine's new book on taking dominion over the night. This is exciting, fresh revelation. I love this book.

—C. PETER WAGNER, CHANCELLOR
WAGNER LEADERSHIP INSTITUTE

In this insightful work, Candi MacAlpine uncovers the spiritual mysteries of the night—revealing why the purposes of God and those of Satan war during those dark hours between sunset and sunrise. *Take Back the Night* will challenge you to awake and redeem all that the enemy has robbed while you were sleeping.

—CHERYL SACKS
COFOUNDER, BRIDGEBUILDERS
INTERNATIONAL LEADERSHIP NETWORK
AUTHOR, *THE PRAYER SATURATED CHURCH*

In her book, *Take Back the Night*, Candi MacAlpine brings forth a powerful revelation of the working of the Lord during the night. Her understanding of the function of the physical body during sleep helps us understand how we are to function spiritually. Hearing God's voice in the night helps us discover God's strategy, brings healing, reveals mysteries, and numerous other benefits. I highly recommend this book to anyone who wants to participate in God's blessings in the night.

—BARBARA WENTROBLE
FOUNDER, INTERNATIONAL BREAKTHROUGH MINISTRIES
AUTHOR, *PROPHETIC INTERCESSION*
AND *PRAYING WITH AUTHORITY*

Candi MacAlpine has uncovered a biblical truth that many American Christians have forgotten. As we reclaim the discipline of fasting, so too must we reclaim the secret power of the night watch. I pray that this book will encourage extraordinary prayer so that the church will truly invade the darkness and claim nations for Christ.

—J. Lee Grady, Editor
Charisma Magazine

Take Back
the
Night

Candi MacAlpine

TAKE BACK THE NIGHT by Candi MacAlpine
Published by Creation House
A Strang Company
600 Rinehart Road
Lake Mary, Florida 32746
www.creationhouse.com

This book or parts thereof may not be reproduced in any form, stored in a retrieval system, or transmitted in any form by any means—electronic, mechanical, photocopy, recording, or otherwise—without prior written permission of the publisher, except as provided by United States of America copyright law.

Unless otherwise noted, all Scripture quotations are from the Holy Bible, New International Version. Copyright © 1973, 1978, 1984, International Bible Society. Used by permission

Scripture quotations marked NLT are from the Holy Bible, New Living Translation, copyright © 1996. Used by permission of Tyndale House Publishers, Inc., Wheaton, IL 60189. All rights reserved.

Scripture quotations marked KJV are from the King James Version of the Bible.

Cover design by Karen Grindley

Copyright © 2005 by Candi MacAlpine
All rights reserved

Library of Congress Control Number: 2004117099
International Standard Book Number: 1-59185-733-3

05 06 07 08 09 — 987654321
Printed in the United States of America

This firstfruit is dedicated to Don, my husband of forty years, who has always been my number one support, always believing in me, especially when I didn't believe in myself or the destiny God had ordained for me. It is with great honor and respect this book is dedicated to him.

Contents

	Foreword by Dr. Bill Hamon	viii
	Introduction	1
1	The History of the Night	3
2	Nightie Night—the Purpose of Sleep	6
3	The Purpose of God	12
4	Creation	19
5	God Speaks About the Night	21
6	God Speaks in the Night	25
7	Dreams and Visions	28
8	The Watches	35
9	War Strategy	40
	Appendix	45
	Notes	55

Foreword

andi has done some wonderful research and writing concerning the night! God created the night as well as the day. In this book you will discover that many good things happen during the night, but also many evil things take place during the dark hours of the night.

The night belongs to the Lord the same as the day. Jesus prayed all night several times before He was to make major decisions and ministry.

The nighttime can be used mightily especially by intercessors who know their authority in Christ Jesus. The reader will gain a greater understanding and appreciation for God's purpose for the night. The powers of darkness have sought to dominate the nighttime. But now God is raising up an army of warrior intercessors who will take back the night for it really belongs to God.

—Dr. Bill Hamon
Chairman/Founder and Bishop
Christian International Ministries Network
Apostle over Christian International Apostolic Network
President, Christian International School of Theology

Introduction

One day, during my morning time with the Lord, I heard Him say, "Take back the night; it belongs to me." I did not think too much of it at the moment, but almost a year later, in my quiet time, I was reading Psalm 74. In verse 16 I read, "Both day and night belong to you; you made the starlight and the sun" (NLT). It really attracted my attention. After repenting for my disobedience to the word I had previously received from the Lord, I began to research the subject of the night. I was utterly amazed at what treasures began to unfold before my eyes. From this point I began walking through experiences that showed me the value and importance of the entire season of the night. The Lord wanted to redeem His purposes, as stated in His Word. It is from this point that we begin this journey into the night and into His light. I pray His light will be shed abroad in your hearts and minds, and that you too will take up the call of God in this hour.

Chapter 1

The History of the Night

In an article written in Charisma *magazine, in February 2002, George Otis Jr. stated:*

> Islam's spiritual DNA is both ancient and troubling. Its primary emblem, the crescent moon, is derived from the Babylonian moon god whose suggestive nickname, "The Controller of the Night," is surpassed only by its formal appellation, "Sin."[1]

The ancient Hebrew and Greek definitions and understandings are a good place to start our foundational structure. *Nyx* is the Greek word for night and refers to the goddess of night. It appears, among other things, as the mother of the Furies. *Nyx* is also the time for magic and the moon goddess, who favors sorcery.

In the Old Testament Hebrew it is a simple indication of time, referencing Genesis 7:4, also hour of terror (Isa. 17:14), a time of drunkenness (Gen. 19:33), sexual misdeeds (Judges 19:25), murder (Neh. 6:10), and occult practices (1 Sam. 28:8). By night man is particularly prone to worry and to the attacks of the evil one (Job. 7:3; Ps. 6:6). But *nyx* is also God's time, when He shows the way by a pillar of fire (Exod. 13:21), makes Himself known in dreams (Gen. 20:3) and visions (Zech. 1:8). At the last day, when salvation is filled, there will be no more night (Zech. 14:7). Nighttime is the time for activity of divine powers. It is at night that angels perform their services (Luke 2:8; Acts 5:19; 12:7; 27:23). He who clings to Christ is no longer under the curse of night (1 Thess. 5:5).

Wow! This is certainly some food for thought, and we have only just begun.

In gnosticism the concept of darkness becomes an independent force, seen as the unlimited ruler of the earthly world. The key to the Old Testament view of light and darkness is faith in God as Creator, who stands above both. He is not only the Lord of light; darkness also has to bow before Him. God makes use of darkness. There is still the promise of Isaiah 9:2 that the people who walk in darkness shall see a great light.

The Old Must Come Down Before the New Can Be Built

When Nehemiah came to rebuild the walls of Jerusalem, he first had to remove the debris of the old structure before he could rebuild the walls and fortify them against the attacks of the enemy who wanted to overtake the city. We are to walk that path and symbolically tear down broken-down walls, so that we can clarify the issue of intercession in the night. We have been walking in the prayer movement for some years now. God has guided us on a path He wants us to tread—that of praying and interceding for our cities as well as our families and personal needs. As we continue to build the walls of prayer around our earth, we are generating a people of promise and purpose to see God's Great Commission fulfilled in the earth. This

The History of the Night

tool of evangelism will add to the arsenal the Lord has provided for us to see victory after victory.[2]

My desire is that God will open our eyes to a deeper understanding of His call for us to take godly dominion of all things upon the earth. My hope is that you will be led to a higher understanding and revelation of the night and its purposes in prayer. I have complemented some scriptures with testimonies of praying people, their personal experiences of nighttime prayer, and the fruit that came from their intercession.

For Further Thought

1. What additional history can you find about the night?

2. What must come down in you before you can receive and act on the revelation of the land of night?

Chapter 2

Nightie Night—the Purpose of Sleep

I researched the subject of sleep, looking for the pattern the Creator has designed for humanity. I sensed there was a connection between sleep and intercession in the night. The more we understand about a subject, the more we are able to evaluate and make decisions based on that understanding.

The Lord led me down this path through a medical process. I was directed by my physician to have a sleep study. The technician who did the study was a Christian friend, and he gave me information about sleep and its purposes in the body. I was fascinated, and as a result, came to recognize a strategy the enemy has used against mankind for centuries. It made me angry at the way the enemy had duped us into believing that he had one up on us. How many times have you been awakened in the night, unable to move or speak? We have usually assumed it was the enemy, and he was

Nightie Night—the Purpose of Sleep

stopping us from moving or speaking. We have usually tried to say "in the name of Jesus," and the words just wouldn't come forth. The enemy was counterfeiting God's authority. One fact I learned from my sleep study is the physiological truth that at the deepest sleep level, our body does, in fact, become paralyzed. The reason for this is that the body is in its deepest level of physical, mental, and emotional healing and restoration. The human body is truly a miraculous machine that is designed with greater excellence than we could ever understand. Wow, what a revelation! A few days later I went to my local library and began researching sleep. Below is a portion of the information I found.

In his book, *The Human Body—Respiration*, Dr. Peter Sebel writes: "General anesthesia causes the brain to go into extremely deep sleep; the respiration center of the brain is depressed and no longer sends nerve signals to the muscles of the respiratory system to contract and move the pump. When this 'deep sleep' is induced by anesthesia, the respiratory pump function must be taken over by a machine pump to support ventilation."[1]

Dr. Martin Hughes, writing in the book, *Body Clock,* says, "Body temperature falls, and the pineal gland releases the hormone melatonin into the bloodstream, which tells the brain and body it is dark and time for transition."[2]

The book *The Promise of Sleep* states that "child" sleep is the "first deep sleep of night; the body secretes a pulse of growth hormone, building new tissue for the growing body, and rebuilding damaged tissue." In stage 4 "all voluntary muscles become completely paralyzed." One is awakened repeatedly during the night to come up for air like a porpoise. During the REM period, "in early morning hours the levels of a hormone called cortisol start rising in the bloodstream. Cortisol is released during times of stress, but the main job now is to mobilize energy stores, preparing the body for the demands of the coming day."[3]

These physiological truths cause me to raise my hands and clap to the Father of all creation for the incredible bodies He has given us. He has made us much more complex than we can understand.

From this knowledge we can learn how we are to function on earth in our mortal bodies.

Night Study

Now let's look at a deeper study of the word *night* as it is used in the Word of God. The *Dictionary of New Testament Theology* states several things about night, but I will share just a few. "Night represents the absence of light, which leaves room for evil and sin. It is a time of refreshment in sleep. Night has usually been given a negative character. Night is ominous and brings fear."[4] It is from this crossroad that we must come higher and look to the Word of God, to see His design for prayer and intercession and His perspective on the night.

I believe the Father has given us a mandate to restore that which was stolen. He is raising up an army to hear and obey His mandate, "Take back the night; it belongs to Me." I believe we will see the level of intercession in the night take a dramatic upswing, and we will see churches, ministries, even cities, facilitate in the night hours what has been practiced in the daylight hours.

Back to Nehemiah

I see a picture in the Book of Nehemiah. The remnant of Israel was in great trouble and disgrace. They were walking in the fruit of their disobedience to God. Something needed to change, and Nehemiah was God's man of the hour.

> The LORD did not set his affection on you and choose you because you were more numerous than other peoples, for you were the fewest of all peoples. But it was because the LORD loved you and kept the oath he swore to your forefathers that he brought you out with a mighty hand and redeemed you from the land of slavery, from the power of Pharaoh king of Egypt. Know therefore that the LORD your God is God; he is the faithful God, keeping his covenant of

Nightie Night—the Purpose of Sleep

love to a thousand generations of those who love him and keep his commands.
—Deuteronomy 7:7–9

Nehemiah reminded God of His promise. He knew the God of covenant and truth, and he understood that God's love for those who obey Him is great. Nehemiah identified with the sin of the people and put himself in their place, executing repentance for them. He had sinned, and because he was an Israelite, he confessed his own sin, and also the sins of the whole remnant in Judah. Even though he wasn't personally responsible for the sins of his ancestors, he could stand in the gap and identify with their sin. He could ask God's forgiveness for their past sins. Nehemiah couldn't even begin to rebuild the walls of Jerusalem until he had gone to the root of sin in the city.

I believe we have given the nighttime over to the enemy. Sin always likes to hide in the dark, and we have allowed it to stay there, because we have not fully taken the land of the night hours. I believe we need to eradicate some roots that are hidden in the night.

Nehemiah was the cupbearer to the King. He had an understanding of the land and the reason for its desolation. Before going to the one in authority, he identified with the sin of the people and repented for them, thus preparing the way for the next step. He had an investment in the city. His forefathers were buried there, and because of their sin, the city was in the hands of the enemy. We are cupbearers of the King of kings, and we have come to an understanding of the land and its desolation. We have gone many places to identify with the sins of past generations. I believe it is now being revealed that the way has been prepared to take another step. The night is part of creation, and as we will see in the pages ahead, an awesome "land" God has created for the purposes of His kingdom. We are the people He is calling to rebuild the "walls."

When we walk according to God's principles, He will always send supplies and reinforcements with us, to help us take the land of night back and restore it. The enemy will always stir things up when God's authority comes on the scene. I look forward to the spoils of the night.

Going undercover to survey the land in the night hours is not such a bad idea; in fact, there is much wisdom in such a strategy. We do not usually need to be in a hurry. It is good to take a team of a few trusted men and women.

The Good News and the Bad News

Nehemiah told his companions the bad news first; then he gave them the good news of God's grace on him and the blessings of the king. I believe we too are standing at that place where we have the blessings of the King to take this territory. "Ites" of one kind or another will always give us headaches. However, I want to remind us that we are the "Joshua-and-Caleb generation." There are giants in the land, but they are small in comparison to the fruit of the land and the milk and honey waiting for us on the other side of the Jordan River. A variety of people rebuilt the gates. We need all personalities to complete the work. Nehemiah fulfilled his purpose in his generation. We want to fulfill our purpose in our generation.

The Stars of the Night

Here, for the sake of this book, are the seven facets of the night. Let's call them the seven stars of the night:

1. The purpose of God
2. Creation
3. God speaks about the night
4. God speaks into the night
5. Dreams and visions
6. The watches of the night
7. War strategy

Nightie Night—the Purpose of Sleep

For Further Thought

1. What has the Lord been speaking to you about the nighttime?

2. Do your own word study about the night. What did you find?

3. What sins of your past generations, personally, or your city can you identify with? Ask forgiveness to see God heal your family or city.

Chapter 3

The Purpose of God

Because the LORD *kept vigil that night to bring them out of Egypt, on this night all the Israelites are to keep vigil to honor the* LORD *for the generations to come.*
—EXODUS 12:42

It was the Jewish Passover, a time of great remembrance for the Israelites. The Lord loved Israel and still does. In this scripture we see the heart of the Father God keeping vigil over His precious children. It was also a historical time, the end of over 430 years of bondage. Can you imagine what was going on in heaven at this late night hour, when the people of God had finally come to the end of their years of struggling? We strive to be free from bondage, and here we see it taking place in the night hours. Stop and ponder for a moment: how many times have you seen breakthrough happen in your life in the evening hours?

Though you probe my heart and examine me at night…
—PSALM 17:3

The Purpose of God

How many times have we sat up late at night, when everyone has gone to bed, and pondered who we are and where we are? It is a time of *examination*. Something about the night lends us to examine our hearts, our motives, and our actions, from either the previous day or other times in our lives. It is a time to set in order things that may be out of order.

> ...to proclaim your love in the morning and your faithfulness at night.
> —Psalm 92:2

During their time in the tabernacle, worshipers were playing instruments and proclaiming God's faithfulness. We can enter into the awesome presence of the Lord twenty-four hours a day, seven days a week, through the ministry of harps and bowls—worship and intercession that has risen up across the body of Christ. It is a time to proclaim God's faithfulness, one of His most important character traits in our lives.

Testimony of His Faithfulness

My friend Bonnie knows firsthand the faithfulness of her Lord. She writes:

> It was the summer of 1991. My youngest daughter Shelly and her friend Dara, who was staying the night, had gone out for the evening with some of their friends. I went to bed and was awakened around 11:00 p.m. I heard the words, *car wreck, car wreck*! I had peace, but I felt an urgency to pray, so I did. I asked the Lord to protect the girls and keep them safe. I then went back to sleep in peace. The next morning, the girls came in for breakfast. I asked Shelly, "Did something happen around 11:00 p.m. last night?" She had the most surprised look on her face and said, "Mom, you must have been praying; a semi-truck almost ran us off the highway."

Take Back The Night

Faithful is He who has called us!

> In the night I remember your name, O Lord, and I will keep your law.
> —Psalm 119:55

This is the most awesome strategy. Enclosed at the end of this book is a list of the names of Jesus in Scripture. Pastor Sam Sasser, a precious man of God, compiled it. Sam was a pastor and a missionary who impacted the Micronesian islands for many years. It is said that *Samuel*, in honor of Sam, is the most common name given to children in Micronesia. I have arisen at night and just sat, proclaiming the names of Jesus into the atmosphere. There is power in the tongue. It is an awesome instrument of warfare, a double-edged sword that will cut and divide the enemies in the night, as we declare the names of the Lord. Books with the names of the Father, using Hebrew names, are also available. You might compile your own list of the names of God. No special anointing or training is required. Just open your mouth and declare Christ's name, and watch the atmosphere over your city change.

> My soul yearns for you in the night; in the morning my spirit longs for you.
> —Isaiah 26:9

In the King James Version the word *desired* is used instead of *yearns*. Its connotation is passion—lust for, to have a desire to be with. How lovely is our yearning for the Lord in the night hours! It leads us in paths of righteousness.

Seed Time and Harvest Principles

> Night and day, whether he sleeps or gets up, the seed sprouts and grows, though he does not know how.
> —Mark 4:27

The Purpose of God

This is an incredible picture of seedtime and harvest. Our family lives in agricultural territory, where planting, growing, and harvesting are always before us. Farmers will tell you that the night hours are imperative for the growing season. The night hours have an integral part in the growth of the plant to become a product that can be harvested. A chemistry change, something very distinct and necessary, takes place during the night hours, and only then. How many times have you, in your own garden, planted either flowers or vegetables? You watch for weeks and see nothing. One night you go to bed, and the next morning you find a sprout, the beginning of fruit on the plant. What an incredible word picture of God's design! Nighttime is a part of the spiritual harvest, and we need to make sure that we follow God's strategy in the night hours to bring forth the harvest of souls. As we pray in the night hours, we are preparing the harvest.

Anna Never Stopped

> There was also a prophetess, Anna, the daughter of Phanuel, of the tribe of Asher. She was very old; she had lived with her husband seven years after her marriage, and then was a widow until she was eighty-four. She never left the temple but worshiped night and day, fasting and praying.
> —Luke 2:36–37

This is the story of Anna the prophetess, who spent her entire life, day and night, worshiping, fasting, and praying in the temple. According to the Law of Moses, parents were required to consecrate every firstborn male child to the Lord. When Joseph and Mary brought Jesus to the temple and did this, Anna was there and was prepared. Simeon prophesied over Jesus, and Anna also came to them and gave thanks to God for the Christ child and declared what the Lord had already revealed to her years before. She knew of the Savior who would be born. Did she hear in the night hours what few knew of the coming Messiah?

Jesus' Ministry in the Temple

> Each day Jesus was teaching at the temple, and each evening he went out to spend the night on the hill called the Mount of Olives.
> —LUKE 21:37

Jesus had stepped into the season of His ministry on earth. He knew He had only so much time to teach the principles of the kingdom of God. Every day He taught in the temple, and each night He went out to the Mount of Olives and spent the night there. Now we can determine that possibly He was just going there to sleep for the night, since the Word tells us He had no place to lay His head (a home to live in). May I suggest, however, that He went to that strategic place each and every night to talk with His Father and receive direction for the next day's teaching? Remember, He told them He only did and said what the Father was doing and saying. He went to that place each evening to get the "word of the Lord" for the following day.

Everything Jesus did while He walked on this earth teaches us and provides an example of how to walk as a Christian. Many times He did things that just pass us by. We have a written record of the ministry direction He received from the Father in the night hours and then walked out during the day. These gems of guidance are not written in sequence, but are the practical way of the kingdom of God. We must personally dig them out and then do likewise.

An Angel Opens a Door

> So Peter was kept in prison, but the church was earnestly praying to God for him.
> —ACTS 12:5

In this instance the night hours were the time of rescue. This is the story of the imprisonment of Peter. His friends were in a home

The Purpose of God

praying for Peter to be freed. It was nighttime, and all of a sudden at the jailhouse, an angel appeared. He opened the prison doors and, low and behold, Peter got up in amazement, and walked out of the cell. Suddenly Peter was alone. He then went to the house where the believers were praying for him. He knocked on the door. As they opened the door, in shock, they saw what they thought was Peter's angel.

The following story parallels the above scripture. In April 2003, during the initial days of the war in Iraq, Jessica Lynch, a young private from Palestine, West Virginia, was taken captive by the Iraqi forces. She had been injured and was housed in an Iraqi hospital. Her family and the townspeople of her home community began having prayer meetings every night at the home of her sister. American Special Forces somehow found out where she was and went in and rescued her. This is the report from her family: "We all jumped up and grabbed each other, hugging everybody and giving thanks to our merciful Lord. Our prayers came through." It is an interesting point that the Special Forces went in to rescue Jessica during the night, using night vision goggles. We need to grab onto that and begin to use spiritual night vision goggles to see what is happening in the night.

Constant Worship in Heaven

> Each of the four living creatures had six wings and was covered with eyes all around, even under his wings. Day and night they never stop saying: "Holy, holy, holy is the Lord God Almighty, who was, and is, and is to come."
> —REVELATION 4:8

This picture of constant worship in the throne room of heaven is familiar to most. Did you ever stop to think that God wants worship to be as intense in the night hours as the day hours? This concept of worship at night was not familiar to the church until a few years ago. We now see the ministry of what is called "harps and bowls" in a number of cities. Everyone may not have the same vision, but a common thread can run through each ministry that takes up the call to constant worship. Can you imagine cities across this nation worshiping God day and night? I promise you, this will send the enemy screaming into outer darkness like nothing else!

For Further Thought

1. What has the Father been probing in you lately? And what are you doing about it?

2. Do you have a testimony of His faithfulness at or in the night hours? Write it down and tell someone about it.

3. What seeds have you been planting during the night that need some attention? What seeds are about to sprout?

4. Keep a journal of what the Father is speaking to you in the night hours only. How does it line up with passages in this book or others in the Bible?

5. Begin having a time of worship just in the night hours, anywhere between when it turns dark until daylight. Journal the results in you, in your family, in your church or city.

Chapter 4

Creation

And God said, "Let there be lights in the expanse of the sky to separate the day from the night, and let them serve as signs to mark seasons and days and years."
—Genesis 1:14

God made two great lights—the greater light to govern the day and the lesser light to govern the night. He also made the stars.
—Genesis 1:16

According to Genesis 1, God created the night. It is His, He owns it, and that finishes it. The enemy has trespassed on the night, which belongs to the God of the universe, and we are instructed to return it to its rightful Owner. For far too long we have relegated the night to the demonic realm, and in all reality, a level of fear has kept the church of Jesus Christ from taking back this territory.

In Genesis 1:14 we are told that lights in the sky separate the day from the night. It is the Father's purpose to mark the order of the earth that He has sovereignly created. The day and night serve the Father; they show us the created signs that mark seasons, days, and years. Creation has no problem submitting to the order of God, and it does it in perfect order. We must see night as part of that order.

Two Great Lights

Genesis 1:16 tells us that God made two great lights, one to govern the day and one to govern the night. The principle of authority is found in the word *governs*. As the sun governs during the day, according to the will of the Creator, so also the night is to fulfill the purpose He has for it. God gave it to us for a reason, and we need to utilize the purpose for which it was created in the beginning. That purpose is to take dominion over all the earth, not just the land, but dominion over all that God created. Time was His creation. Therefore we can, in His authority, given by Jesus before He left earth, take dominion over the night.

For Further Thought

1. Do a nature study, even with children, about what happens in nature in the night hours.

Chapter 5

God Speaks About the Night

Do not let this Book of the Law depart from your mouth; meditate on it day and night, so that you may be careful to do everything written in it. Then you will be prosperous and successful.

—Joshua 1:8

When the Lord told Joshua to meditate on His Word day and night, it wasn't because the man did not know the Word. God knew that as Joshua meditated on His Word, it would prepare him for a great purpose. What was that purpose? The call to meditate on the Word day and night was the preparation for Joshua to lead the children of Israel across the Jordan River into the Promised Land, with its milk and honey, and take dominion of it. Israel had been walking through the wilderness for forty years, even though the journey was only supposed to be eleven days or so. We can glean from this scripture that nighttime meditation on the Word brings forth things we do not know. The Father knows what lies ahead, and we need to prepare.

Will You Answer the Call?

> The day is yours, and yours also the night; you established the sun and moon.
> —Psalm 74:16

Here it is—God's voice in the night hours calling us to take back the night. A simple verse written in the poetry of the Psalms, it is a strong statement of God's ownership of the light He created in the beginning of time. It is our clarion call, if you will, to take the land of the night and establish it as the kingdom of our God. There has been a remnant, but it is the hour of the multitudes. This is not something that requires any special location, equipment, music, or leadership. It is a call to the individual first, to establish at home the Father's purposes in the night hours. It is then a battle strategy for establishing the kingdom of God in every arena, every location, every city, state, and nation. The hours of night that have been stolen by the kingdom of darkness will be returned to the kingdom of our God. It is true that evil hides in the darkness, but now we must shine the light of Jesus into that place and establish the lesser light in its destiny.

Will Jesus Return at Night?

> I tell you, on that night two people will be in one bed; one will be taken and the other left.
> —Luke 17:34

This may be poetic wording. Jesus was speaking in this scripture. Was He giving us insight into the time of His return? Will the rapture come during the night hours? We are told to be alert at all times, watching for His return. If we are asleep, spiritually, we could miss His return. Jesus always spoke to the multitudes in parables, but later explained the parables to His disciples. We are His disciples, and we have a responsibility to hear what the Spirit is saying.

"Listen! A farmer went out to sow his seed. As he was scattering the seed, some fell along the path, and the birds came and ate it up. Some fell on rocky places, where it did not have much soil. It sprang up quickly, because the soil was shallow. But when the sun came up, the plants were scorched, and they withered because they had no root. Other seed fell among thorns, which grew up and choked the plants, so that they did not bear grain. Still other seed fell on good soil. It came up, grew and produced a crop, multiplying thirty, sixty, or even a hundred times."

Then Jesus said, "He who has ears to hear, let him hear."

When he was alone, the Twelve and the others around him asked him about the parables. He told them, "The secret of the kingdom of God has been given to you. But to those on the outside everything is said in parables so that, 'they may be ever seeing but never perceiving, and ever hearing but never understanding; otherwise they might turn and be forgiven!'"

Then Jesus said to them, "Don't you understand this parable? How then will you understand any parable? The farmer sows the word. Some people are like seed along the path, where the word is sown. As soon as they hear it, Satan comes and takes away the word that was sown in them. Others, like seed sown on rocky places, hear the word and at once receive it with joy. But since they have no root, they last only a short time. When trouble or persecution comes because of the word, they quickly fall away. Still others, like seed sown among thorns, hear the word; but the worries of this life, the deceitfulness of wealth and the desires for other things come in and choke the word, making it unfruitful. Others, like seed sown on good soil, hear the word, accept it, and produce a crop—thirty, sixty or even a hundred times what was sown."

He said to them, "Do you bring in a lamp to put it under a bowl or a bed? Instead, don't you put it on its stand? For whatever is hidden is meant to be disclosed, and whatever is concealed is meant to be brought out into the

open. If anyone has ears to hear, let him hear."
—Mark 4:3–23

Jesus told His disciples some things are meant to be hidden, and those who are of His kingdom must search to find these hidden truths. He promised that what was concealed was meant to be brought into the open. I believe now is the time for us to search for the hidden truths of the night. I am not setting the time of Christ's return. I believe this is a hidden truth that applies to the purpose of nighttime intercession and warfare strategy. The night watches are part of this purpose.

Job Cries Out in the Night

But no one says, "Where is God my Maker, who gives songs in the night?"
—Job 35:10

Elihu responded to all that Job and his three friends said and refers to what I believe was the testimony of his own troubled times. He was testifying of how God had met him in his distress in the night hours, and with that meeting came songs of praise and worship in the midst of the trials. There is something about that cloak of darkness—the lesser light, as Genesis says—that gently brings out of our innermost being wonderful ministries from the Lord.

For Further Thought

1. Go outside at night and just look up into the night and meditate on the night sky, journal what you see and feel and what the Lord reveals.

2. Ponder the times of distress when you have cried out at night, and what the results were. Again journal it, even if it was years ago.

Chapter 6

God Speaks in the Night

But God came to Abimelech in a dream one night and said to him, "You are as good as dead because of the woman you have taken; she is a married woman."
—Genesis 20:3

What a wake-up call! This certainly would awaken you from a deep sleep. We could use many more scriptures, but we are only drawing from a few. It would take hundreds of pages to expound on all of them. Father God speaks strongly to His children in the night hours. In this case, Abraham was on his way to his destiny. However, he became frightened for his own life, and he lied. The Lord was not happy, so He spoke to Abimelech. It did not make any difference if the king knew God. He heard the clear, strong voice of God awaken him, to tell him He was not happy with his plan to sleep with Sarai. Remember, God knows the heart of every man and woman, and this was no place to mess with the purposes of God. Aren't we glad Abimelech responded correctly!

That night the Lord appeared to him and said, "I am the God of your father Abraham. Do not be afraid, for I am

> with you; I will bless you and will increase the number of your descendants for the sake of my servant Abraham."
> —Genesis 26:24

Isaac had come to Beersheba. He had suffered problems in the days past—arguments with the Philistines, who had filled his father's wells with dirt—as he struggled with his destiny. But on this one night at Beersheba, God awakened Isaac and brought encouragement to him. Isaac knew that his father was an incredible man of God. He knew of the promises the Lord had made to him. He knew of the friendship his father had with God. That could have been intimidating, and it probably was. He was a young man, learning the ways of life. Isaac needed to hear about his purpose on earth from God Himself.

The Lord came to Isaac that night and said, "You're Abraham's son, and I promised your father he would have multitudes of descendants." God may have continued the dialogue by saying something like this: "You are next in line, and that same promise flows through your loins. I sent you to this new place, and I know it's different. It can be frightening, but I have sent you here to see the promises continue. You must redig the wells of your father. They have been contaminated and polluted by your enemies."

The enemy will fill our wells with sand and do everything he can to discourage and distract us from our destiny. There will always be Philistines lurking around the corner, spying on our walk with God, and trying to gum up the works of the fullness of God's destiny for us.

> On that same night I will pass through Egypt and strike down every firstborn—both men and animals—and I will bring judgment on all the gods of Egypt. I am the Lord.
> —Exodus 12:12

This was Israel's time. It had come. All the trials, the persecutions, the backbreaking labor for the Egyptians had finally come to an end. God had declared, "It is time for my people to come up

God Speaks in the Night

and out of Egypt. The entire nation of Egypt and all Israel will now see that I am the true God. They will not be able to reject this move of My hand."

God sent the angel sweeping through Egypt, killing every firstborn, all the way up to Pharaoh. The only exceptions were the Israelites who had marked their doorways with the blood of a sacrificed lamb, so that the angel of death would pass over them.

This was a time in history that the children of Israel would never forget. In fact, they would remember it for all time. It remains a Jewish ceremony of the Exodus and is remembered every year. It was a time of release, a time of destiny for their nation.

For Further Thought

1. What bad things have happened in your city during the night hours? Get some statistics and begin to get the strategy to change or even eliminate those statistics.

2. Begin to think about, "Has God been speaking to me at night?"

Chapter 7

Dreams and Visions

Joseph Has a Visitation

Each of the two men—the cupbearer and the baker of the king of Egypt, who were being held in prison—had a dream the same night, and each dream had a meaning of its own.

—Genesis 40:5

This well-known story of Joseph and his journey of destiny from his birth to his death gives us one of the great examples of the purpose of God for a man, his generations, and a nation. Joseph was one the Lord singled out to hear His plans and purposes by receiving spiritual dreams. He was not wise in his younger years and told his brothers about dreams that showed them being subservient to him. Since he was much younger than they were, his nighttime

Dreams and Visions

revelations caused them to resent him and his dreams. They were so enraged that they sold him into slavery, to stop his talk about all his "ridiculous" dreams. In spite of Joseph's lack of wisdom, God used his foolishness to fulfill His purposes for him, as well as his family and ultimately the children of Israel.

We hear about Joseph and dreams again when he is in prison. While he worked as a slave in charge of Potiphar's household, Potiphar's wife took a liking to him and tried to seduce him. After being falsely accused by her and then thrown into prison, he encountered two men who had worked in the king's palace, the chief baker and the chief cupbearer to the king. The Lord has a way of putting us right where He wants us so that He can prepare us for our destiny, even though it seems like we are in the worst place possible. The baker and the cupbearer each had a dream one night and told Joseph about their respective dreams the next morning. Since he was in a state of confinement already, he might as well utilize his ability to interpret dreams, so he mentioned to them that he can tell them what their dreams mean. God gave him the interpretation of the dreams, and he asked the cupbearer to remember him when he was restored to his position.

The Lord may put us in places we think are unjustifiable, but we usually cannot see the bigger picture or the plan that lies ahead. Be open to nighttime dreams that are directional for yourself, or for others. Everyone has dreams that are significant; we just do not realize their importance, unless we have searched out information that teaches about the interpretation of dreams.

Can a Nonbeliever Have a Spiritual Dream?

As we see in the story of Joseph and the king's workers, you do not have to be Christian for the Lord to speak to you in a dream. An unbeliever may be thoroughly confused about the meaning of a dream. If we have become equipped in understanding dreams and the language of dreams, we can help lead that person to a saving knowledge of Jesus Christ.

> And God spoke to Israel in a vision at night and said, "Jacob! Jacob!" "Here I am," he replied. "I am God, the God of your father," he said. "Do not be afraid to go down to Egypt, for I will make you into a great nation there."
> —Genesis 46:2–3

In this vision, God promises to make Jacob a great nation. Well, why not? This is an awesome way for God to gain our attention. Jacob was a bit prone to being here and there, doing this and that. This dream may have been the only way the Lord could get his full attention. We may be in that same state, and the Lord will use that time when our body is being restored and refreshed to speak our destiny into us through dreams.

My own testimony of God's call on my life came initially through a dream I had over twenty-five years ago. I was a young Christian, in an evangelical church, serving and pursuing God with all my heart. Because I had no idea that God spoke through dreams or any other way except the Bible, it did not really impact me at the time it happened. I saw myself dressed in a white robe-like garment. I was in a church that was not familiar to me, and I was preaching. I was quoting scriptures I did not know at the time, but I knew they were the Word of God. It was very vivid. However, I did not think about the dream for over fifteen years.

When the Lord called me to ministry ten years ago, He brought that dream back to my remembrance, as vivid as it had been the night it came. I realized the Lord had spoken to me of His call for me to serve Him and the body of Christ, even though I had no understanding of what He was saying at the time.

Solomon's Wake-up Call

> At Gibeon the Lord appeared to Solomon during the night in a dream, and God said, "Ask for whatever you want me to give you."
> —1 Kings 3:5

Dreams and Visions

What a wake-up call this was for Solomon! The Lord had told David, Solomon's father, that his son would be a great man of God, and that he would be wiser than any man alive then or later. This is the kind of statement you might think would come to Solomon through a prophet during the day, but the Lord chose the night. God had Solomon's full attention, and He knew that Solomon would not choose unwisely. Wow! I want that kind of interaction with my heavenly Father.

A Laser Beam Healing

Let me share a dream I had several years ago. I was attending a Wagner Leadership Institute fast track on prophecy in Colorado Springs, Colorado. During the night I had a dream about a leader I knew. In the dream, I saw him at a distance from me and witnessed a laser beam go from what I determined to be the Lord to the inside of his left knee. I had no idea what this meant. The next morning I arrived for my class about fifteen minutes early. I wanted to see if he was teaching a class that day, and, lo and behold, he was. I went to his classroom, and asked if he had a moment. After I told him about my dream, I asked him if he had a problem with his left knee. He said, "Yes, I do." When I asked if it was the inside of his left knee, he replied, "Yes, it is; that is amazing. I have an old football injury there, and it has been bothering me for some time. I have gone to an orthopedic surgeon, and he wants to do surgery on my knee. I have not told anyone about this situation. The doctor wants to do surgery very soon. After the doctor's appointment, the Lord said, 'Have you asked Me about this, and if I was going to heal it?'" The leader concluded, "This is my answer." God was going to heal the knee injury by His laser beam.

What a blessing it was for me to be able to communicate this dream and the promise of healing to this child of God! I know it was no coincidence that I was in Colorado and he just happened to be teaching a class where I was.

A Spirit of Death Is Stopped in Its Tracks

> In a dream, in a vision of the night, when deep sleep falls on men as they slumber in their beds, he may speak in their ears and terrify them with warnings, to turn man from wrongdoing and keep him from pride, to preserve his soul from the pit, his life from perishing by the sword.
>
> —Job 33:15–18

This story comes from the chief intercessor of a well-known ministry:

> When our first daughter was about one year old, she woke up screaming at the top of her lungs. She normally slept through the night. It was about 11 p.m. There was something in her cry that made us think it was more than just the natural baby cry. Both my wife and I could also discern the presence of evil in our home. I began to pray earnestly in the Spirit and battle against this evil, while my wife tried to comfort our daughter. She went down the list of things that makes an infant cry and none of them applied. Then we received a phone call from the president of our ministry who was ministering in Atlanta with his wife. They were rushing his wife to the emergency room because she had nearly fainted and was feeling extremely dizzy and couldn't breathe properly. We realized that this was an attack of witchcraft, and we were standing in the gap for them. Our daughter had discerned the evil spirit, which is why she woke up screaming. I continued to pray along these lines, and after about a half-hour we felt the evil spirit leave, and the presence of the Lord filled our home. Our daughter also stopped crying and went peacefully back to sleep. We then worshiped the Lord for a while, and went back to sleep ourselves. A little while later we were awakened by a phone call from our president's secretary saying that the attack had been broken (about the same time we had felt the breakthrough), and the doctor found nothing wrong and had sent them home.

Dreams and Visions

We must be discerning when we are awakened in the night hours. The Lord sends His strategies in the night hours to combat the enemy's strategy. Our body may go to sleep, but our spirit is forever awake, watching, listening to the Father. He is always ready to communicate to us about an assignment of prayer.

Mysteries Are Revealed in the Night

> During the night the mystery was revealed to Daniel in a vision.
> —Daniel 2:19

This is a simple, but exact passage. Why didn't the Lord reveal it during the daytime hours? He chose to reveal the mystery and the vision to Daniel in the night hours. Many times we struggle with situations, circumstances, or relationships. We pray for answers, and it isn't until we are asleep that the answers come. Many times we may have received answers to situations, but were not aware that the answer came in the night. It is interesting that a thrust of training has come in the area of dreams and visions and the interpreting of dreams and visions. We need to be educated in this arena.

I thank God for those who, like Daniel and Joseph, have a unique anointing and are helping the body of Christ to understand and walk in revelation of their dreams and visions. Resources are available to help you understand and interpret your dreams and visions. The one I use most is *Interpreting the Symbols and Types*.[1]

The Call for Revival Help

> During the night Paul had a vision of a man of Macedonia standing and begging him, "Come over to Macedonia and help us."
> —Acts 16:9

Take Back The Night

This is the well-known Macedonian call for Paul to come and share the gospel with the people in Macedonia. God knows the timing and purpose, when and where, to release the gospel of Jesus into a land. It was evident that this was God's time, and Paul was the man. He had been on his way to Damascus when God struck him down with a great light and vision. This was Paul's waterloo. Jesus captured his heart and set him into his destiny.

The Macedonian call is another vision invasion, but this time Paul was not dumbfounded. He knew who was speaking, and he knew where he was to go with the gospel. How many of us have had similar experiences and didn't realize we were being called to a city, or even a nation? It may have been so preposterous that we just thought it was a result of the pizza we ate for dinner.

For Further Thought

1. Are you keeping a journal of your dreams?

2. Take a class, get some books, go to a seminar or conference on dreams and dream interpretation. Get knowledge of this form of communication from the Lord. Use it as an evangelistic tool to win people to the Lord.

Chapter 8

The Watches

Because a number of books have been written about the watches of the night, we will not spend a great deal of time rehashing this area. I want to add, nonetheless, a few of the scriptures that reference the watches of the night.

The watches consisted of four segregated times: 9 p.m. to midnight (first), midnight to 3 a.m. (second), 3 a.m. to 6 a.m. (third), and 6 a.m. to 9 a.m. (fourth). The Jews had three watches until Roman times. The Romans, being strong rulers, changed the number of watches to four, and that is how they continue to be observed today.

Doorkeepers of the Lord

They would spend the night stationed around the house of God, because they had to guard it; and they had charge

of the key for opening it each morning.
—1 Chronicles 9:27

Those who were musicians, heads of Levite families, stayed in the rooms of the temple and were exempt from other duties because they were responsible for the work day and night.
—1 Chronicles 9:33

The musicians and heads of families who were responsible for the house of God were told to stay in their house during the night hours. They were assigned to stand at the doors of the temple and keep guard. I wonder what they experienced in that time with the Father. I wonder what we would experience if we stationed ourselves at the doorway of our churches during the night hours. I know we have used this figuratively in prophetic acts and have seen situations change because the enemy was not allowed to enter a gateway.

Praise the Lord, all you servants of the Lord who minister by night in the house of the Lord.
—Psalm 134:1

A blessing is released over those who are called to minister in the night. I am sure part of that blessing is the ability to stay awake and be able to function the following day. One of my key intercessors is a watchman. She has a full-time job during the day. On many occasions she will be awake during the night, interceding for two, four, or even six hours. She will awaken at her regular hour, go to work, and be fine during the day. That definitely is a blessing—and a miracle in my book.

On my bed I remember you; I think of you through the watches of the night.
—Psalm 63:6

My eyes stay open through the watches of the night, that I may meditate on your promises.
—Psalm 119:148

The Watches

These scriptures give a distinct direction for what we are to do. The writers of these psalms, anointed by the Holy Spirit, wrote not only to give instruction, but to testify of what they were doing in the night hours. Meditating on the promises of God in a quiet setting like the night is an act of intimacy with God. It releases faith and hope in our troubled times. What a time to just ponder the things of God! Noise has decreased, all in the household are asleep, and we can just remember the hundreds of promises that belong to us as children of the King.

> And the lookout shouted, "Day after day, my lord, I stand on the watchtower; every night I stay at my post."
> —Isaiah 21:8

This is one of the greatest admonishments to those called to the watchman anointing. It is a mighty call with a great deal of responsibility, and it takes place predominantly in the night hours.

> I have posted watchmen on your walls, O Jerusalem; they will never be silent day or night.
> —Isaiah 62:6

It is evident from this scripture that the watchman doesn't sit quietly on the wall, but that he is engaged in activity that does not include silence. The intercessor I mentioned above has consistently heard the Lord direct her to pray for specific situations regarding people, cities, and nations. After she prayed for one of these situations, she saw a newspaper report about it.

The Storms Will Rage in Our Lives

> During the fourth watch of the night Jesus went out to them, walking on the lake.
> —Matthew 14:25

Take Back the Night

I always ask why some scriptures are in the Bible, and this is one of them. I don't believe it was placed there just to say there were watches. It tells of a time when Jesus went out to the disciples with a specific purpose—to give them another test in their school of discipleship. This is one of the most familiar scriptures, where we focus on Peter and his walking out to Jesus on the water.

I believe we can look deeper and find another nugget of purpose. The night watches are a time when Jesus wants to come and visit us in a most dramatic, dynamic way. In this scene Peter and the other disciples had to make a choice. They were challenged to get out of the boat and walk in faith to the Master. Peter was the only one with enough faith to step out and reach for Jesus. They had walked on land with Jesus for some time now. They knew a lot about His character, His activity, and the many miracles He had performed in their midst. But there weren't any crowds around now; it was only Jesus, the disciples, a lake, and a raging storm.

We have a challenge here. Are we willing to get out of the boat to meet Jesus on what in the natural are unstable circumstances? Faith is the key. God has not promised us an easy life without storms, but He has promised He will never leave us or forsake us. He has also promised us His peace, a peace that is not of this world. In fact He is the Prince of Peace, and His peace will guard our hearts and minds as we seek Him.

> It will be good for those servants whose master finds them ready, even if he comes in the second or third watch of the night.
>
> —Luke 12:38

Again we ask, "Why do we have this scripture?" Could it be that Jesus may come in the night hours? I certainly am not suggesting times and dates for the return of Jesus Christ, but I am emphasizing our need to be more focused on spiritual activities, like intercession in the night hours.

The Watches

For Further Thought

1. Find out what your night hours are. Not everyone is called to be a night watchman, and not all nighttime prayer is after midnight.

2. Find out if it is possible to build a nighttime strategy at your church or prayer group. Start small. Do not overwhelm yourself or your leadership.

3. Do your own word study/search to find all that Jesus did in the night hours and apply it to yourself.

4. What do you need to do to get out of the boat?

Chapter 9

War Strategy

By now, many in the body of Christ have come to realize that we are at war, a war that will continue until Jesus returns to take His church into eternity. In the last ten years, we have received a strong teaching emphasis on spiritual warfare from a number of sources. Even though some in the body of Christ have yet to hear of the terminology of spiritual warfare, we have finally embraced this reality and truth.

I remember when it became a reality to me. I was involved in the ministry training of Cleansing Stream Deliverance Discipleship. One of our required readings was C. Peter Wagner's *Prayer Warrior*.[1] I had never heard of the teaching in this book, but it was like fireworks going off in my spirit. I knew this was what I was created for. I had very little understanding of spiritual warfare, but from that point I began to devour every published work I could find. As I look at my library now, surely a fourth of my books cover the subject of prayer and spiritual warfare.

It is, of course, important to see the principles of any theology based on the Word of God, and warfare is no exception. We have now received revelation that directs us to take up the armor of God and the weapons of warfare, in order to establish the kingdom of God wherever we are on the earth.

We have truly received our marching orders, and the Captain of the hosts of the Lord has called us to ride alongside Him at the helm. He reminds us that Revelation 11:15 says, "The kingdom of the world has become the kingdom of our Lord and of his Christ, and he will reign for ever and ever." We will defeat the enemy of God and of our souls. I have read the end of the book, and we win.

It is reported that the main activity of occult powers happens between midnight and 3 a.m. each night. Demonic spirits awaken the servants of Satan, and they prophesy over the star alignments, especially birthdays, and place curses against the church of Jesus Christ. This is just one of Satan's strategies. If he has strategies, we must also have strategies to overcome him. Two great strategies are: "Greater is he that is in you, than he that is in the world" (1 John 4:4, KJV), and "They overcame him by the blood of the Lamb, and by the word of their testimony" (Rev. 12:11, KJV).

Give Me a Strategy!

In this final chapter, the last "star," we will look at five Old Testament scriptures that focus on specific strategies the Lord gave His people to defeat their enemies. The setting for each situation was in the night hours, and great victories were won by God's people when they prayed and obeyed His plans. At times the plans seemed ridiculous to the leaders, and sometimes they didn't obey. As a result of their disobedience, they suffered defeat, the consequence of their choice to disregard the strategy of the Lord. These are only a few of numerous scriptures that give examples of the way the Lord accomplished His will in the midst of rebellion and disobedience by the people of the earth.

> During the last watch of the night [the morning watch] the Lord looked down from the pillar of fire and cloud at the Egyptian army and threw it into confusion.
> —Exodus 14:24

> So Joshua and the whole army moved out to attack Ai. He chose thirty thousand of his best fighting men and sent them out at night with these orders: "Listen carefully. You are to set an ambush behind the city. Don't go very far from it. All of you be on the alert. I and all those with me will advance on the city, and when the men come out against us, as they did before, we will flee from them. They will pursue us until we have lured them away from the city, for they will say, 'They are running away from us as they did before.' So when we flee from them, you are to rise up from ambush and take the city. The Lord your God will give it into your hand. When you have taken the city, set it on fire. Do what the Lord has commanded. See to it; you have my orders."
> —Joshua 8:3–8

> That night the angel of the Lord went out and put to death a hundred and eighty-five thousand men in the Assyrian camp. When the people got up the next morning—there were all the dead bodies!
> —2 Kings 19:35

> "So arise, let us attack at night and destroy her fortresses!" This is what the Lord Almighty says: "Cut down the trees and build siege ramps against Jerusalem. This city must be punished; it is filled with oppression."
> —Jeremiah 6:5–7

> Stay here for the night, and in the morning if he wants to redeem, good; let him redeem. But if he is not willing, as

War Strategy

> surely as the Lord lives I will do it. Lie here until morning.
> —Ruth 3:13

In each of these scriptures the situation was tense, and the lives of people or nations were at stake. I am thankful for people like Joshua, Jeremiah, and Ruth who trusted and obeyed God and at other times did not. The Lord knows our hearts. It is easy to judge a situation after the fact, when all is well. However, in the midst of difficulty—whether it is an Old Testament battle or the struggle for the soul of a child who is in total rebellion against God—we must trust the Lord. He really does know best. The key issue is trust. God leads us in His truth, and we must come to the place of obedience and trust.

In conclusion, you may be at the beginning of your personal quilt of inspiration and strategy for prayer and intercession. Or you may be enlarging your quilt with new pieces. My desire is that you will grasp the nuggets of truth in these pages and pursue another level or arena of prayer in your life. My sole purpose has been for Jesus to be pleased, and the body of Christ to mature in a new level of prayer. I pray that you will realize the Lord of the universe has sovereignly designed your Christian walk to be a partnership with Him.

God does not need us. He certainly could do His work alone, much quicker and better without us, but He has decided that He wants a team to establish His kingdom on the earth He created. We have an awesome opportunity; we are living in the most exciting time of history. We, as never before, have come into an understanding of prayer, intercession, spiritual warfare, and the purposes of God on earth.

I want to be counted in my generation, and if Jesus tarries, I want to give my grandchildren a nation—even an earth—that glorifies God. I want to be remembered for great exploits in my lifetime. I pray an impartation of revelation and activation for nighttime intercession. May your nights be forever changed. May you look at the night as the most incredible opportunity to see the kingdom of this world become the kingdom of our God.

For Further Thought

1. Whether you want to or not you are called to war and to be a warrior. Find your place in the ranks of God's nighttime army.

2. Ask the Lord for your personal strategy, or for your group.

3. Find all the examples of characters in the Bible who were involved with a strategy in the night to overthrow the kingdoms of darkness.

4. Begin to use the appendix at the end of this book, calling out the names of the Lord in Scripture. It is a good starting point for anyone or any group. Be creative.

Appendix

Sam Sasser has compiled this list of the names of Jesus. The scriptures are from the King James Version and the New International Version.

A		B	
Aaron	Heb. 8:5	Babe	Luke 1:32
Abel	Heb. 11:4	Balm of Gilead	Jer. 8:22
Adam	1 Cor. 15:45–47	Banner of nations	Isa. 11:12
Advocate	1 John 2:1	Baptizer	Matt. 3:11–12
All in all	Col. 3:4	Beginning	Rev. 21:6
Almighty	Rev. 1:8	Beginning of creation	Rev. 3:14
Alpha	Rev. 21:6		
Altar	Heb. 13:10	Begotten of God	1 John 5:18
Altogether lovely	Song of Sol. 5:16	Beloved	Eph. 1:6
Amen	Rev. 3:14	Beloved Son	Matt. 3:17
Anchor	Heb. 6:18–19	Bishop of souls	1 Pet. 2:25
Ancient of days	Dan. 7:9	Blessed and only potentate	1 Tim. 6:15
Angel of His presence	Isa. 63:9		
		Branch	Zech. 3:8
Angel, mine	Exod. 23:20–23	Branch of root of Jesse	Isa. 11:1
Anointed above fellows	Ps. 45:7		
		Branch, righteous	Jer. 23:5
Anointed, His	Ps. 2:2	Bread of God	John 6:33
Apostle of our profession	Heb. 3:1	Bread of life	John 6:35
		Bridegroom	Isa. 54:5
Approved of God	Acts 2:22	Bright morning star	Rev. 22:16
Ark	Heb. 11:7		
Arm of the Lord	Isa. 51:9–10	Brightness of His glory	Heb. 1:3
Author and finisher	Heb. 12:2		
		Brother	Mark 6:3
Author of eternal salvation	Heb. 5:9	Bruiser	Gen. 3:15
		Builder	Matt. 16:18
Avenger	Ruth 4:1–8	Bundle of myrrh	Song of Sol. 1:13
Ax	Matt. 3:10		

45

C

Called	Isa. 49:1
Candlestick	Rev. 21:23
Captain of Lord's host	Josh. 5:15
Captain of salvation	Heb. 2:10
Carpenter's Son	Matt. 13:55
Chief among ten thousand	Song of Sol. 5:10
Chief cornerstone	1 Pet. 2:6
Chief shepherd	1 Pet. 5:4
Child	Isa. 9:6
Chosen	Isa. 28:16
Chosen of God	Luke 23:35
Christ chosen of God	Luke 23:35
Christ end of law	Rom. 10:4
Christ head of church	Eph. 5:23
Christ high priest	Heb. 9:11
Christ Jesus our Lord	Rom. 8:39
Christ King of Israel	Mark 15:32
Christ King	Luke 23:2
Christ Messiah	John 1:41
Christ our life	Col. 3:4
Christ power of God	1 Cor. 1:24
Christ Son of God	John 20:31
Christ the firstfruits	1 Cor. 15:23
Christ the Lord	Luke 2:11
Christ, the	John 1:41
Comforter	Isa. 61:2–3
Coming one	Luke 7:19; Rev. 1:4
Commander	Isa. 55:4
Consolation of Israel	Luke 2:25
Consuming fire	Heb. 12:29
Corn of wheat	John 12:24
Counselor	Isa. 9:6
Covenant of the people	Isa. 42:6
Covert	Isa. 4:6
Covert from the tempest	Isa. 32:2
Creator	Isa. 40:28
Creator of all things	Col. 1:16
Creator of ends of earth	Isa. 40:28
Crown of glory	Isa. 28:5
Curse	Gal. 3:13

D

David's son	Luke 20:41
Dayspring	Job 38:12
Delight	Prov. 8:30
Deliverer	Luke 1:78
Desire of all nations	Hag. 2:7
Destroyer	Ps. 2:9
Dew	Hos. 14:5
Diadem	Isa. 28:5
Divider	Luke 12:14
Door, the	John 10:9

E

Elect	Isa. 42:1

Appendix

Elected stone	1 Pet. 2:6
Emmanuel	Matt. 1:23
End	Rev. 1:8
End of law	Rom. 10:4
Ensign	Isa. 5:26
Eternal life	1 John 5:20
Eternally blessed	Rom. 9:5
Everlasting Father	Isa. 9:6
Example	1 Pet. 2:21

F

Faithful and true	Rev. 19:11
Faithful witness	Rev. 1:5
Father	Isa. 9:6
Father of mercies	2 Cor. 1:3
Finisher	Heb. 2:10
Fire	Matt. 3:10-12
First among many brethren	Rom. 8:29
First and last	Rev. 22:13
Firstborn over all creation	Col. 1:15
First begotten	Heb. 1:6
Firstborn	Ps. 89:27
Firstborn from dead	Col. 1:18
Firstfruits	1 Cor. 15:23
Flame	Isa. 10:17
Flesh	Rom. 1:3
Forerunner	Heb. 6:20
Foundation	Isa. 12:3–6
Foundation in Zion	Isa. 28:16
Fountain of living waters	Jer. 17:13–14
Fourth man	Dan. 3:25
Friend	Matt. 11:19
Friend closer than brother	Prov. 18:24
Friend of publicans and sinners	Matt. 11:19
Fruit of the earth	Isa. 4:2
Fulfiller of righteousness	Matt. 3:15
Fullness	Col. 2:9
Fullness of Godhead	Col. 2:9

G

Galilean	Matt. 4:13–16
Garden of renown	Ezek. 34:29
Gift	2 Cor. 9:15
Gift of God	John 4:10
Glorious Lord	Isa. 33:21
Glorious throne	Isa. 22:23
Glory of Israel	Luke 2:32
Glory of the Lord	Isa. 40:5–9
God blessed	Rom. 1:25
God full of compassion	Ps. 86:15
God manifest in flesh	1 Tim. 3:16
God my savior	Luke 1:47
God of all comfort	2 Cor. 1:3
God of glory	Acts 7:2
God of grace	1 Pet. 5:10
God of hope	Rom. 15:13
God of Israel	Isa. 45:15
God of love and peace	2 Cor. 13:11
God of my life	Ps. 42:8

47

Take Back The Night

God of patience and comfort	Rom. 15:5	Head of body	Col. 1:18
God of peace	Rom. 15:33	Head of every man	1 Cor. 11:3
God of recompenses	Jer. 51:56	Head over all things	Eph. 1:22
God of truth	Deut. 32:4	Head stone of corner	Ps. 118:22
God of whole earth	Isa. 54:5	Healer	Isa. 61:1
God the judge of all	Heb. 12:23	Health of my countenance	Ps. 42:11
God with us	Matt. 1:23	Heavenly	John 3:13
Good	Matt. 19:16–17	Heir of all things	Heb. 1:2
Good master	Mark 10:17	Helper	Heb. 13:6
Good shepherd	John 10:11	Herald	Isa. 61:1
Good teacher	Mark 10:17	Hidden manna	Rev. 2:17
Governor	Mic. 5:1	Hiding place	Isa. 32:2
Gracious	1 Pet. 2:3	High and lofty one	Isa. 57:15
Grain of wheat	John 12:24	High priest	Heb. 3:1
Great God	Titus 2:13	Highest	Luke 1:76
Great high priest	Heb. 4:14	Holy	Isa. 57:15
Great King above all gods	Ps. 95:3	Holy and reverend	Ps. 111:9
Great light	Isa. 9:2	Holy and true	Rev. 6:10
Great prophet	Luke 7:16	Holy One and the just	Acts 3:14
Great shepherd of sheep	Heb. 13:20	Holy One of Israel	Isa. 41:14
Greater	John 1:27; Matt. 12:6	Holy thing	Luke 1:35
Green tree	Luke 23:31	Hope of glory	Col. 1:27
Guest	Luke 19:7	Hope of Israel	Isa. 11:1
Guide	Luke 1:79	Hope of our fathers	Jer. 50:7
		Horn of salvation	Ps. 18:2
		Husband	Rom. 7:4

H

Habitation of justice	Jer. 50:7
Harmless	Heb. 7:26
He who lives	Rev. 1:18

I

I am	John 8:58

Appendix

Illegitimate	John 8:41
Image of God	2 Cor. 4:4
Image of invisible God	Col. 1:15
Immanuel	Isa. 7:14
Immortal	1 Tim. 1:17
Innocent	Matt. 17:4
Intercessor	Isa. 53:12; John 17:9
Invisible	John 1:18
Israel	John 1:47; Mic. 4:2

J

Jehovah	Isa. 33:22
Jehovah eternal creator	Gen. 2:4–25
Jehovah Lord my God	Zech. 14:5
Jehovah Lord of hosts	1 Sam. 1:3
Jehovah Lord our banner	Exod. 17:15
Jehovah Lord our God	Exod. 20:2
Jehovah Lord our maker	Ps. 95:6
Jehovah Lord our peace	Judg. 6:24
Jehovah Lord our righteousness	Jer. 23:6
Jehovah Lord our sanctifier	Lev. 20:8
Jehovah Lord our shepherd	Ps. 23:1
Jehovah Lord your healer	Exod. 15:26
Jehovah most high	Ps. 7:17

Jehovah will provide	Gen. 22:8–14
Jesus	Matt. 1:21
Jesus Christ our Lord	Rom. 1:3
Jesus Christ the righteous	1 John 2:1
Jesus of Nazareth	Mark 16:6
Jew	John 4:9
Judge and lawgiver	Isa. 33:22
Judge of Israel	Mic. 5:1
Judge of living and dead	Acts 10:42
Just	Acts 7:52
Just One	Acts 7:52
Justifier	Isa. 50:8

K

King	Zech. 9:9
King in His beauty	Isa. 33:17
King of glory	Ps. 24:7
King of Israel	John 1:49
King of kings	Rev. 17:14
King of peace	Heb. 7:2
King of saints	Rev. 15:3
King over all earth	Zech. 14:9
King's son	Ps. 72:1
Kinsman	Isa. 59:20

L

Lamb of God	John 1:29
Lamb slain	Rev. 5:12

49

Take Back The Night

Lamb without blemish	1 Pet. 1:19	Lord Jesus Christ our Savior	Titus 1:4
Last	Rev. 1:11	Lord Jesus Christ, Son of the Father	2 John 3
Lawgiver	James 4:12		
Leader	Isa. 55:4	Lord mighty in battle	Ps. 24:8
Liberty	Isa. 53:7-9		
Life	John 14:6	Lord most high	Ps. 47:2
Life-giving spirit	1 Cor. 15:45	Lord of all	Acts 10:36
Light of city	Rev. 21:23	Lord of all the earth	Zech. 6:5
Light of Gentiles	Isa. 42:6		
Light of Israel	Isa. 10:17	Lord of glory	1 Cor. 2:8
Light of men	John 1:4	Lord of harvest	Matt. 9:38
Light of the morning	2 Sam. 23:4	Lord of living and dead	Rom. 14:9
Light of the world	John 8:12	Lord of lords	1 Tim. 6:15; Rev. 17:14
Lily of the valleys	Song of Sol. 2:1	Lord of peace	2 Thess. 3:16
Lion	Heb. 7:13	Lord of the Sabbath	Matt. 12:8
Lion of Judah	Rev. 5:5		
Living bread	John 6:51	Lord our maker	Ps. 95:6
Living one	Rev. 1:18	Lord our redeemer	Isa. 43:14
Living stone	1 Pet. 2:4	Lord our righteousness	Jer. 23:6
Living way	Heb. 10:20		
Lord and Christ	Acts 2:36	Lord strong and mighty	Ps. 24:8
Lord and God	John 20:28		
Lord and Master	John 13:13	Lord who created the heavens	Isa. 45:18
Lord and Savior Jesus Christ	2 Peter 1:11		
		Love	1 John 4:8
Lord Christ	Col. 3:24	Lover	Song of Sol. 1:16
Lord from heaven	1 Cor. 15:47		
Lord God Almighty	Rev. 4:8	# M	
		Majesty	Heb. 1:3, 8:1
Lord God of truth	Ps. 31:5	Maker	Isa. 45:11
Lord God omnipotent	Rev. 19:6	Maker of all things	Jer. 51:19
Lord Jesus	Acts 1:21	Man	John 6:52
Lord Jesus Christ	Acts 11:17		

Appendix

Man approved by God	Acts 2:22
Man of sorrows	Isa. 53:3
Man of war	Exod. 15:3
Manna	Exod. 16:15
Master	Matt. 23:10
Master of the house	Luke 13:25
Mediator	1 Tim. 2:5
Mediator of a better covenant	Heb. 8:6
Mediator of the new covenant	Heb. 12:24
Meek	Matt. 21:5
Melchizedek	Ps. 110:4
Messenger	Mal. 3:1
Messiah	John 1:41
Mighty God	Isa. 9:6
Mighty One	Ps. 45:3
Mighty One of Israel	Isa. 30:29
Mighty One of Jacob	Isa. 60:16
Minister of the sanctuary	Heb. 8:2
Morning star	Rev. 2:28
Morning without clouds	2 Sam. 23:4
Most high	Ps. 18:13
Most Holy	Dan. 9:24
Most mighty	Ps. 45:3
Mountain	Dan. 2:35
My beloved	Matt. 12:18
My elect one	Isa. 42:1
My fortress	Ps. 18:2
My glory	Ps. 3:3
My help	Ps. 115:11
My helper	Heb. 13:6
My high tower	Ps. 144:2
My hope	Ps. 71:5
My lamp	2 Sam. 22:29
My Lord and my God	John 20:28
My portion	Ps. 73:26
My power	2 Sam. 22:33
My righteous servant	Isa. 53:11
My salvation	Ps. 38:22
My shield	2 Sam. 22:3
My song	Isa. 12:2
My strength	Ps. 59:9
My strength and my song	Isa. 12:2
My strong rock	Ps. 31:2
My support	Ps. 18:18
My well beloved	Isa. 5:1

N

Nazarene	Matt. 2:23
Numbered with the transgressors	Isa. 53:12

O

O Lord God of hosts	Ps. 59:5
Offering	Eph. 5:2
Offering for sin	Isa. 53:10
Offspring	Zech. 6:12
Ointment poured forth	Song of Sol. 1:3
Omega	Rev. 21:6
One I love	Song of Sol. 3:2
One shepherd	John 10:16

51

One who shall have dominion	Num. 24:19	Prince of the kings of the earth	Rev. 1:5
Only begotten of the Father	John 1:14	Prophet	Deut. 18:15–18
Only wise God	1 Tim. 1:17	Propitiation	Rom. 3:25
Ordained	Acts 10:42	Propitiation for our sins	1 John 2:2
Our great God	Titus 2:13	Purifier	Mal. 3:3
Our hope	1 Tim. 1:1		
Our lawgiver	Isa. 33:22		

R

Our passover	1 Cor. 5:7	Rabbi	John 1:49
Our peace	Eph. 2:14	Rabboni	John 20:16
Our potter	Isa. 64:8	Rain	Hos. 6:3
		Rain upon the mown grass	Ps. 72:6

P

Passover	1 Cor. 5:7	Ransom	Matt. 20:28
Peace	Isa. 9:6	Redeemer	Isa. 59:20
Peace offering	Lev. 3:1–5	Refiner	Matt. 3:10–12
Pearl	Matt. 13:46	Refuge	Isa. 4:6
Perfect	Luke 6:40	Rest	Matt. 11:28
Physician	Luke 4:23	Restorer	Ps. 23:3
Plant	Ezek. 34:29	Resurrection	John 11:25
Portion of Jacob	Jer. 10:16	Revealer	Luke 10:21
Portion of mine inheritance	Ps. 16:5	Rewarder	Heb. 11:6
		Rich	2 Cor. 8:9
Potter	Isa. 44:2	Righteous	Luke 23:47
Power	1 Cor. 1:24	Righteous judge	2 Tim. 4:8
Preacher	Isa. 61:1–2	Righteous servant	Isa. 53:11
Precious	1 Pet. 2:4	River	Isa. 32:2
Precious stone	1 Pet. 2:6	Rivers of water	Isa. 32:2
Priest	Heb. 2:17	Rock	1 Cor. 10:4
Priest forever	Heb. 5:6	Rock of my salvation	2 Sam. 22:47
Prince	Deut. 9:25	Rock of offence	1 Pet. 2:8
Prince and savior	Acts 5:31	Rock that is higher than I	Ps. 61:2
Prince of life	Acts 3:15		
Prince of peace	Isa. 9:6	Rod	Isa. 11:1
Prince of princes	Dan. 8:25		

Appendix

Rod from the stem of Jesse	Isa. 11:1	Shepherd who died	Matt. 26:31
Rod of thy strength	Ps. 110:2	Shield	2 Sam. 22:31
		Shield of thy help	Deut. 33:29
Root of David	Rev. 5:5	Shiloh	Gen. 49:10
Root of Jesse	Isa. 11:10	Sign	Luke 2:34; Matt. 12:38
Root out of dry ground	Isa. 53:2	Smitten shepherd	Zech. 13:7
Rose of Sharon	Song of Sol. 2:1	Soap	Mal. 3:2
Ruler	Mic. 5:2	Son	1 John 4:14
		Son of David	Matt. 12:23
		Son of God	Rev. 21:7; Rom. 1:4

S

Sacrifice	Heb. 11:4	Son of Joseph	John 1:45
Salvation	Isa. 62:11	Son of man	Acts 7:56
Same	Heb. 13:8	Son of Mary	Mark 6:3
Sanctification	1 Cor. 1:30	Son of the Highest	Luke 1:32
Sanctuary	Isa. 8:14		
Savior of the world	1 John 4:14	Son of the most high God	Mark 5:7
Scapegoat	Lev. 16:1–34	Sower	Matt. 13:37
Sceptre	Num. 24:17	Standard	Isa. 62:10
Sealed	John 6:27	Star out of Jacob	Num. 24:17
Seed of David	John 7:42	Stone	Matt. 21:42
Seed of the woman	Gen. 3:15	Stone cut without hands	Dan. 2:34
Servant	Isa. 42:1–4	Stone of Israel	Gen. 49:24
Shadow	Isa. 4:6	Stone of stumbling	1 Pet. 2:8
Shadow from the heat	Isa. 25:4		
		Stranger	Matt. 25:35–44
Shadow of a great rock	Isa. 32:2	Strength	1 Sam. 15:29
		Strength of my life	Ps. 27:1
Shepherd	Heb. 13:20		
Shepherd of Israel	Ps. 80:1	Strength of the Children of Israel	Joel 3:16
Shepherd of your souls	1 Pet. 2:25	Strong Lord	Ps. 89:8
		Stronghold	Nah. 1:7

53

Strong tower — Ps. 61:3
Sun and shield — Ps. 84:11
Sun of righteousness — Mal. 4:2
Supreme — Rom. 9:5
Sure foundation — Isa. 28:16
Surety — Heb. 7:22
Sword of thy excellency — Deut. 33:29

T

Tabernacle — Isa. 4:6
Teacher — John 3:2
Temple — Rev. 21:22
Testator — Heb. 9:16
Thief — 1 Thess. 5:2–4
Thing (Holy) — Luke 1:35
Tower of salvation — 2 Sam. 22:51
Trap and snare — Isa. 8:14
Treasure — 2 Cor. 4:7
Tree — Luke 23:31
Tried stone — Isa. 28:16
True bread from heaven — John 6:32
True God — 1 John 5:20
True Light — John 1:9
True — John 5:20
Truth — John 14:6

U

Understanding — Prov. 8:14
Unspeakable gift — 2 Cor. 9:15
Upholder of all things — Heb. 1:3

V

Veil — Heb. 10:20
Vine — John 15:1

W

Water — John 4:10–14
Way — John 14:6
Wonderful — Isa. 9:6
Word coequal — John 1:1
Word eternal — John 1:1
Word of God — Rev. 19:13
Word: Creative — John 1:3
Crowning — Rev. 19:13
Illuminating — John 1:7
Incarnate — John 1:14
Powerful — Heb. 4:12
Revealing — John 1:18
Superior — John 1:15–17

Y

Yea — 2 Cor. 1:20
Your confidence — Prov. 3:26
Your everlasting light — Isa. 60:20
Your exceeding great reward — Gen. 15:1
Your Holy One — Acts 2:27
Your keeper — Ps. 121:5
Your King — Zech. 9:9
Your Maker — Isa. 54:5
Your shade — Ps. 121:5
Your shield — Gen. 15:1

Notes

Chapter 1
The History of the Night

1. George Otis Jr, *The Mysterious World of Islam, Charisma & Christian Life,* February 2002, 40.
2. Colin Brown, ed., *New International Dictionary of New Testament Theology,* volume 1 (Grand Rapids, MI: Zondervan, 1975, 1986), 420–425.

Chapter 2
Nightie Night—the Purpose of Sleep

1. Peter Sebel, *The Human Body—Respiration* (New York: Torstar Books, Inc., 1985), 62.
2. Martin Hughes, MD, *Body Clock* (Oxford, UK: Andromeda Oxford, 1989), 79–83.
3. William C. Dement, MD, PhD, and Christopher Vaughan, *The Promise of Sleep* (NY, NY: Delacorte Press, Random House, 1999), 21–22.
4. Colin Brown, ed., *New International Dictionary of New Testament Theology,* 220.

Chapter 7
Dreams and Visions

1. Kevin J. Connor, *Interpreting the Symbols and Types* (Portland, OR: BT Publishing, 1980).

Chapter 9
War Strategy

1. C. Peter Wagner, *Prayer Warrior* (Ventura, CA: Regal Books, 1990).

To Contact the Author

Candi MacAlpine is available to minister in your church, ministry, or nation. You may contact her at:

P.O. Box 2285
Oakhurst, CA 93644
(559) 683-6774
E-mail: dtc@sti.net
Web site: www.destinytc.com